For little explorers

Vinci Press

rachelvinciguerra.com/author

USA - Canada - UK -Australia - India - China etc.

Ordering Information:

Special discounts are available on quantity purchases by schools, nonprofits, and others.

For details, contact the publisher at the url address above.

For orders by bookstores and wholesalers, please order through the Ingram Content Group and ipage.

First Edition: February 2021

Library of Congress Control Number: 2020914063

Vinciguerra, Rachel, 1992- author.

Spirit and Oppy : Have you heard the story of the twin sisters who explored the surface of Mars?

They were NASA's twin rovers, Spirit and Opportunity (or Oppy for short)--

ISBN 978-1-7358506-1-0 (hardcover)

ISBN 978-1-7358506-2-7 (paperback)

ISBN 978-1-7358506-3-4 (ebook)

[1. Space-Nonfiction. 2. Science-Nonfiction. 3. Grief and Loss-Fiction.] I. Gottwalt, Samantha, 1994 -illustrator. II. Spirit and Oppy

Designed by Samantha Gottwalt - Text set in Josefin Sans

Illustrations were created using paper cutting and collage.

Science Advisor: Tanya Harrison, PhD (tanyaofmars.com)

NASA technology represented with permission from NASA.

Spirit and Oppy

By Rachel Vinciguerra

Illustrated By Samantha Gottwalt

Vinci Press
Pittsburgh, PA

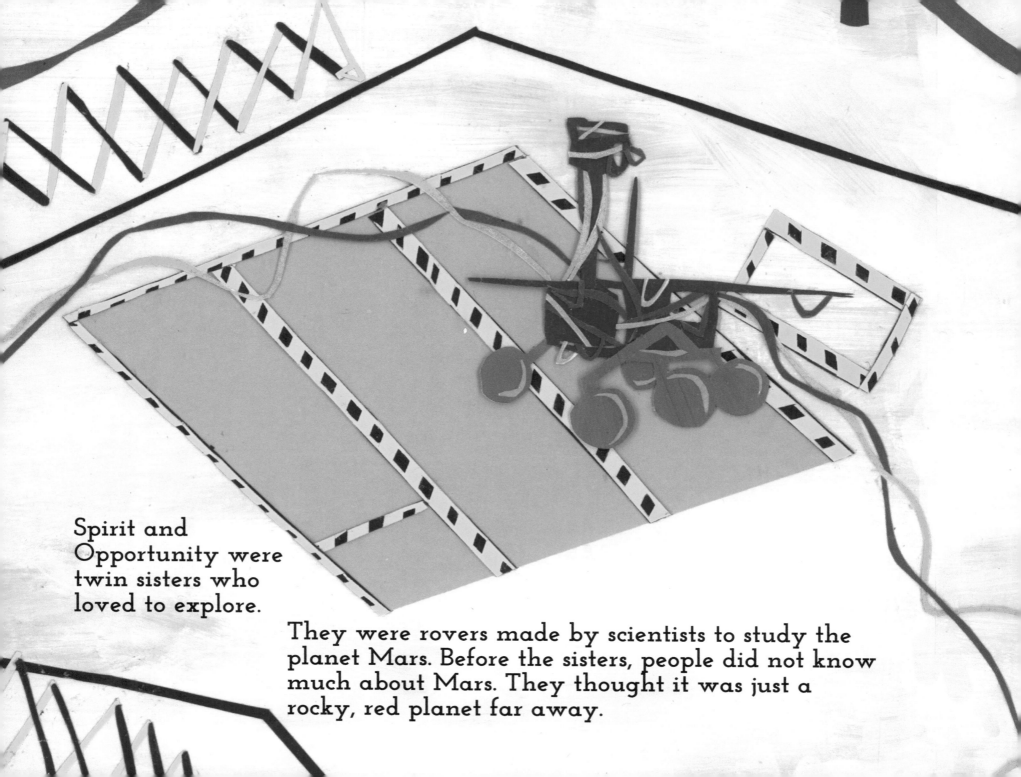

Spirit and Opportunity were twin sisters who loved to explore.

They were rovers made by scientists to study the planet Mars. Before the sisters, people did not know much about Mars. They thought it was just a rocky, red planet far away.

On a hot summer afternoon in 2003, hundreds of people watched from Earth as Spirit took off in a fiery rocket. On an even hotter day, a month later, Opportunity followed.

The scientists called her Oppy for short.

Three months passed as Spirit and Oppy zoomed through space, alone in their modules. Until one day they arrived and descended to the red planet.

Each rover carried big balloons that filled with air right before she reached the hard ground on Mars. When Spirit hit the surface, she bounced and bounced and then settled peacefully on the ground like a snowflake.

She was excited to land in a crater where she found rocks with small holes and lots of minerals. She sent pictures and measurements back to Earth. When they saw the pictures, the scientists thought, *these rocks look like they came from volcanoes.*

Oppy landed in a much smaller crater on the opposite side of the planet. She wondered about the smaller, rounder rocks she found. They made the scientists on Earth think of blueberries. *Maybe the minerals in these rocks came from water,* the scientists thought. They imagined tiny organisms on Mars once upon a time.

Each sister carried solar panels on her back. The panels caught the sun's rays, turning them into energy for Spirit and Oppy to move around the planet.

The scientists thought Spirit and Oppy's mission would last for 90 days. But the sisters were determined to explore for far longer. They had to find out if Mars once had water like Earth. Their exploration turned from days, into months, and then years.

Spirit sent photographs of Mars to Earth. In her photos, the people saw a vast horizon with rocks, dust, and her wheel tracks behind.

Both rovers used their robot arms and drills to pick up and study soil. Oppy even found salt near the crater where she landed. The scientists imagined there had once been a wide lake in its place.

It was not always easy, but the sisters kept going. When Spirit's solar panels were covered by dust, she waited patiently for the wind to blow it off so she could charge. When there were problems with Oppy's right wheel, she drove backwards with help from the scientists on Earth. Even though she couldn't see ahead, she knew she had to keep going.

Through their exploration, Spirit and Oppy learned that Mars was not just a rocky, red planet like the people once thought. It was covered with sand and dust and plains too.

The sisters explored together for five years on opposite sides of the planet. Until one day, the people on Earth heard that Spirit was stuck. Her wheels were wedged in the sand where the sun could not reach her solar panels and give her energy. Some of the people were sad her mission was done.

But they were happy
to know that Oppy
was still exploring,

leaving big wheel
tracks in the dust
behind her.

As ten more years passed, Oppy continued her work, traveling farther on the planet than anyone or anything had outside of Earth. Until one day, a radio announcer shared news about Oppy again.

He said she had been on the edge of the Endeavour Crater when a powerful dust storm hit.

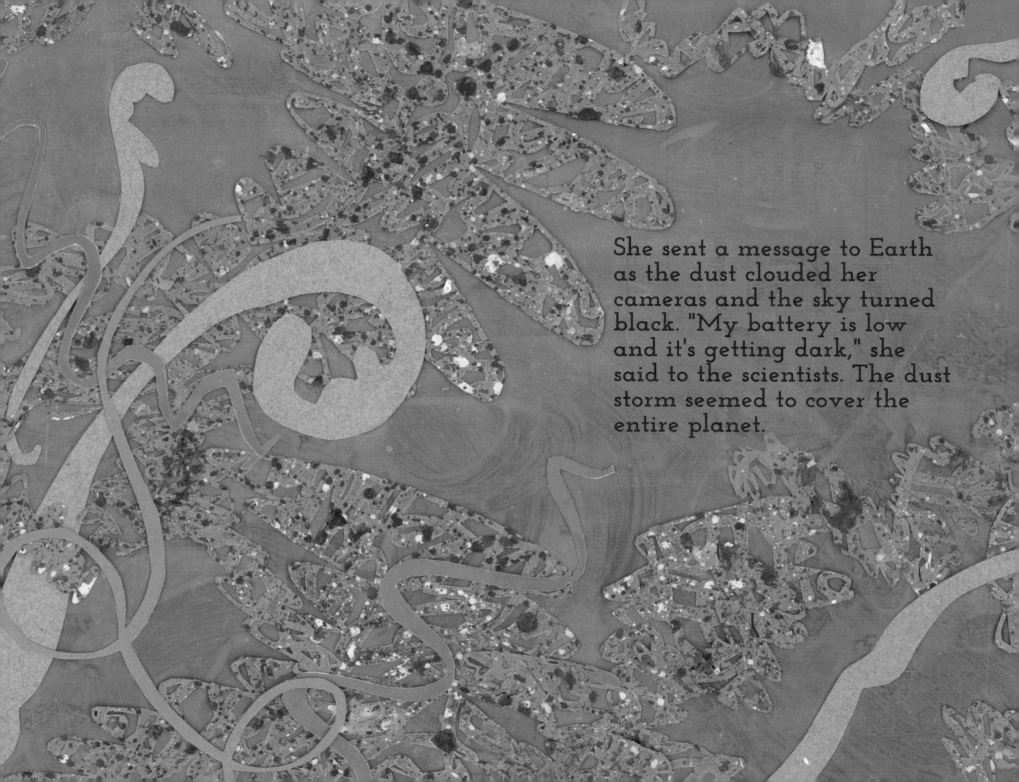

She sent a message to Earth as the dust clouded her cameras and the sky turned black. "My battery is low and it's getting dark," she said to the scientists. The dust storm seemed to cover the entire planet.

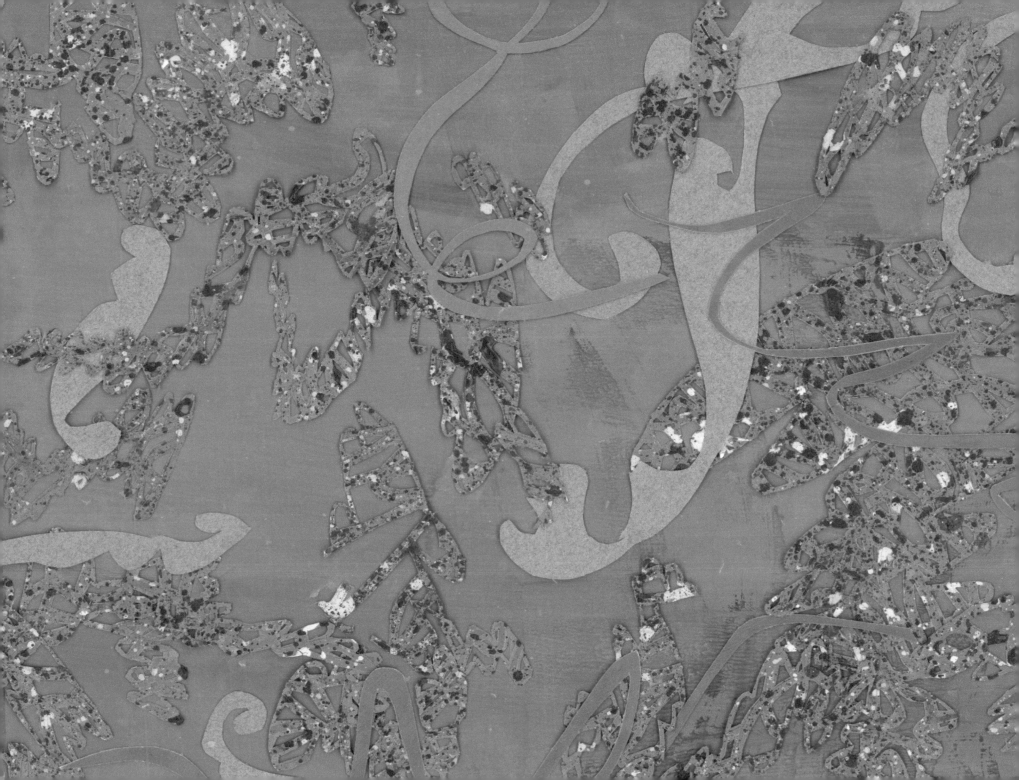

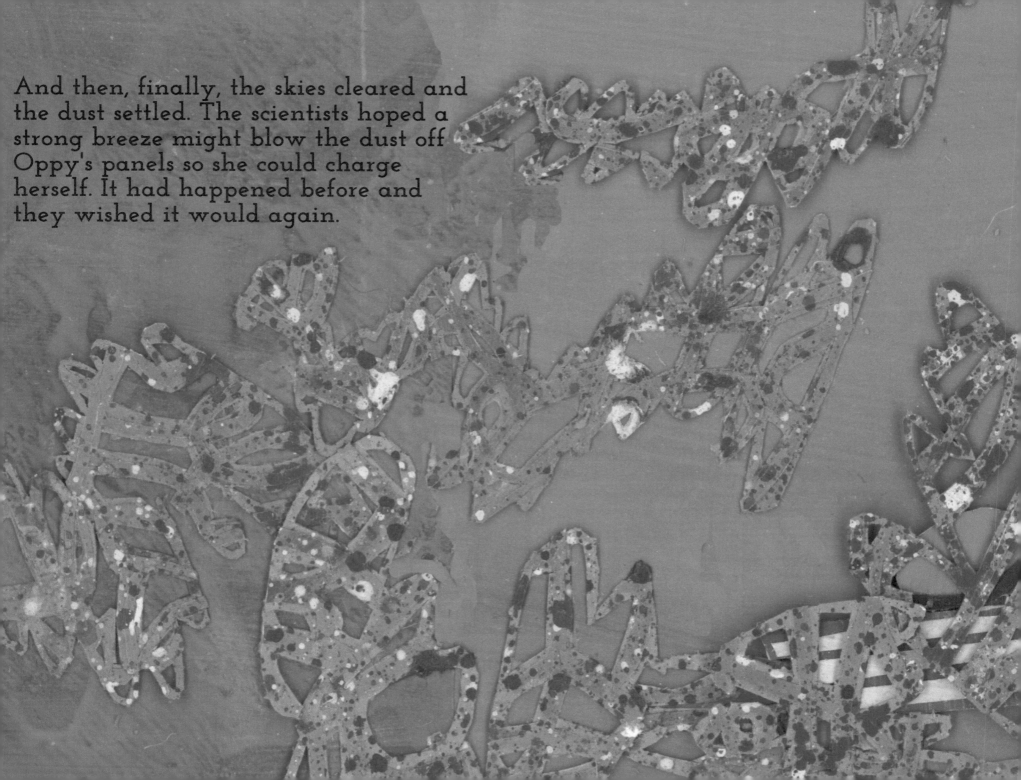

And then, finally, the skies cleared and the dust settled. The scientists hoped a strong breeze might blow the dust off Oppy's panels so she could charge herself. It had happened before and they wished it would again.

They tried to communicate with her. They wanted very much to save Oppy and studied her design to see if there was some clue to wake her up. They even sent Oppy messages they thought would do the trick. When the messages did not work, they played her music. But Oppy could not reply.

The scientists knew her battery was dead. She had no more energy. To say goodbye, they played her one last song.

...I'LL BE SEEING YOU, IN

Billie Holiday's gentle voice carried across the universe to Oppy.

When the song finished, the lead scientist told the others that Oppy was gone. They would not send her another message. She had been bold in her mission. And people all over the world saw Mars through her eyes.

Because of Spirit and Oppy, we know that Mars was once warm, that there was water . . . and maybe even life.

The twin rover sisters reminded the people on Earth how much we don't yet know. Their exploration created a spark of an idea for the scientists to PERSEVERE and use their INGENUITY to always keep exploring.

Glossary

Geologist: A geologist is a scientist who studies solid, liquid, and gas elements that make up the terrain on the Earth and other planets. Spirit and Opportunity were geologists on Mars.

NASA: NASA is the National Aeronautics and Space Administration in the United States. Its mission is to pioneer the future in space exploration, scientific discovery, and aeronautics research. NASA started Mars Missions that included Spirit and Opportunity.

Mars: Mars is known as the "red planet" and is the easiest planet to access from Earth. Once every 18 months or so, Mars is close enough for a rocket to travel to the surface. It is the fourth planet away from the sun and is relatively small compared to other planets. Mars has winds and weather similar to Earth. Unlike Earth, the atmosphere is very thin and mostly made of carbon dioxide with only a small amount of oxygen and water vapor. Mars also has two moons!

Opportunity: One of the twin Mars Exploration Rovers, Opportunity, launched on July 7, 2003 from Earth and landed in the Meridian Planum on January 25, 2004. Opportunity explored the planet Mars and sent signs of life back to Earth. She last communicated with Earth on June 10, 2018 when a dust storm covered the planet and NASA's last attempt at communication came in February 2019. Her mission lasted for 15 years.

Perseverance & Ingenuity: The newest Mars Exploration Rover, Perseverance, launched on July 30, 2020. Perseverance traveled with a small helicopter called Ingenuity and the two are expected to land on Mars in February 2021 and spend at least one year on their mission.

Rover: A rover is a special vehicle that allows scientists to explore the surface of planets and other terrain in space. Sometimes rovers carry human crews and other times rovers operate alone and send measurements and photographs back to Earth.

Spirit: One of the twin Mars Exploration Rovers, Spirit, launched on June 10, 2003 from Earth and landed in Gusev Crater on January 4, 2004. Spirit explored the planet Mars for six years.

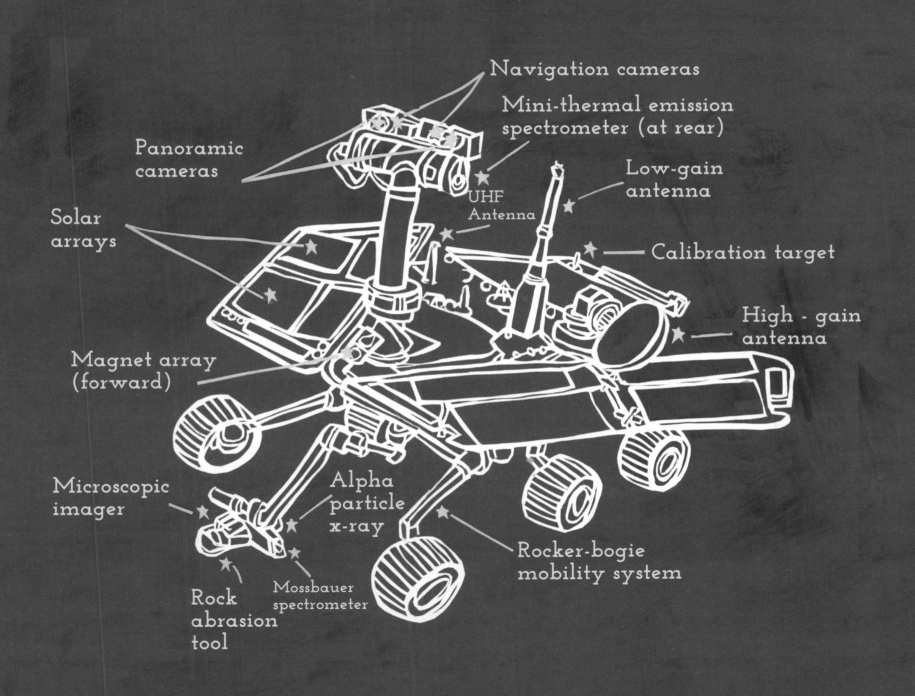

Navigation cameras

Mini-thermal emission
spectrometer (at rear)

Panoramic
cameras

Low-gain
antenna

Solar
arrays

UHF
Antenna

Calibration target

High - gain
antenna

Magnet array
(forward)

Microscopic
imager

Alpha
particle
x-ray

Rocker-bogie
mobility system

Rock
abrasion
tool

Mossbauer
spectrometer

Author's Note

When Spirit and Oppy launched in 2003, I was 11 years old. My parents have always loved space exploration and my sister and I were fortunate they shared this love with us through the Mars Rovers. I remember my excitement for the rovers to land on Mars and how I studied the landing gear with my dad to present to my 5th grade class.

Over the years, the rovers sent back incredible photographs of the planet and took measurements of rocks and soils that indicated a high likelihood of livable conditions on Mars. What were intended as 90-day missions remarkably turned into 6 years for Spirit and 15 for Opportunity.

As those years passed, the rovers sank into the recesses of my memory. It wasn't until NASA declared Oppy's mission complete in February 2019 that my recollections came flooding back. I was surprised how affected I was hearing the news of NASA's final attempt to communicate with Oppy by playing Billie Holiday's "I'll Be Seeing You." It touched my heart because it reminded me of an important time in my life as a little girl learning with my family and imagining possibilities for my life, our universe, and each other.

Even today I get excited about the Mars Missions! I cannot wait to see what Perseverance and Ingenuity will discover next.

About the Author

RACHEL VINCIGUERRA is a first-time children's book author, social worker, and yoga instructor. She manages the Hello Neighbor Network, a national network of grassroots organizations supporting refugees. She lives in Pittsburgh with her cat, Zéb, and some chickens.

rachelvinciguerra.com

@rachelvinciguerra

About the Illustrator

SAMANTHA GOTTWALT is an illustrator and collage artist living in Portland, Maine. When she's not cutting and gluing paper, she enjoys trying new recipes, traveling with her husband, and cuddling with her kitty, Jiji.

scgottwaltillustration.com

@samanthacarolli

GEMIN

VASTITAS

ARCADIA
PLANITIA

ACIDALIA
PLANITIA

EAESUS MONTES

ALBA
MONS

TEMPE
TERRA

CHRYSE
PLANITIA

AMAZONIS
PLANITIA

URANIUS
MONS

OLYMPUS
MONS

ASCRAEUS
MONS

LUNAE
PLANUM

XANTHE
TERRA

PAVONIS
MONS

ALLIS

ARSIA
MONS

VALLES MARINERIS

LUCUS
ANUM

SYRIA
PLANUM

DAEDALIA
PLANUM

SINAI
PLANUM

SOLIS
PLANUM

THAUMASIA
PLANUM

MA

TERRA

BOSPOROS
PLANUM

SIRENUM

ICARIA
PLANUM

ARGYRE
PLANITI

AONIA
TERRA

AONIA

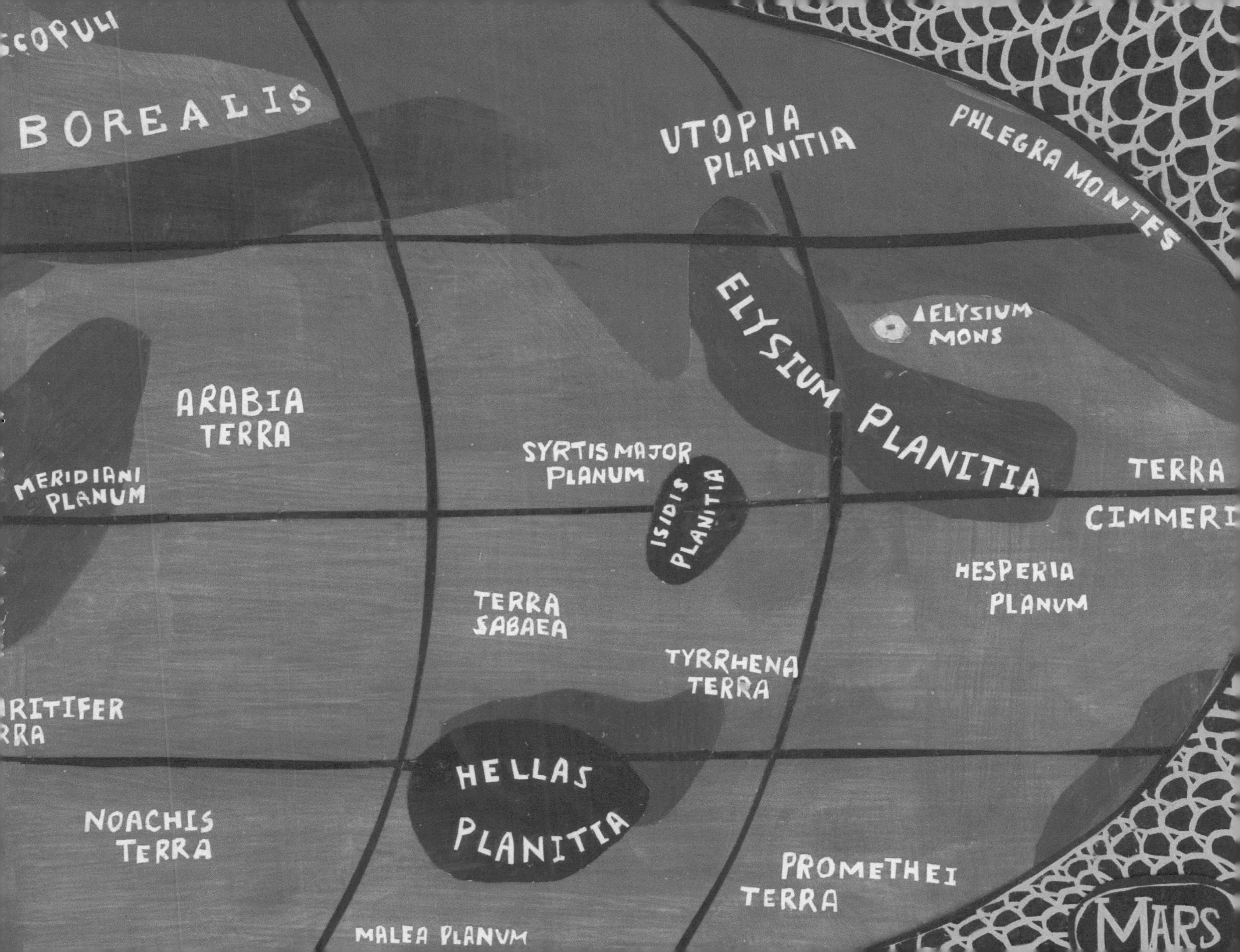
SCOPULI
BOREALIS
UTOPIA PLANITIA
PHLEGRA MONTES
ELYSIUM PLANITIA
ELYSIUM MONS
ARABIA TERRA
MERIDIANI PLANUM
SYRTIS MAJOR PLANUM
ISIDIS PLANITIA
TERRA CIMMERI
HESPERIA PLANUM
TERRA SABAEA
TYRRHENA TERRA
RITIFER
RRA
HELLAS PLANITIA
NOACHIS TERRA
PROMETHEI TERRA
MALEA PLANUM
MARS

Printed in the USA
CPSIA information can be obtained
at www.ICGtesting.com
LVHW061348251023

761976LV00021B/448